This is the story of Kirk Gibson. His attempt to win a game is one of baseball's most courageous moments.

In the 1988 World Series, the Los Angeles Dodgers faced the Oakland Athletics. Most fans were convinced that the Athletics had the best chance to win. Oakland had good pitchers and great hitters.

The Dodgers also had good pitchers and great hitters. But they had a big problem. Kirk, their best player, had a serious leg injury. He could not run. He could hardly swing a bat! No one thought Kirk would recover in time to play in the World Series.

The first game was played in Los Angeles. Early in the game, Oakland was ahead. The Dodgers finally began to catch up as the end of the game approached. They needed two more runs to win the game. With only three outs left, their chances of winning were not good.

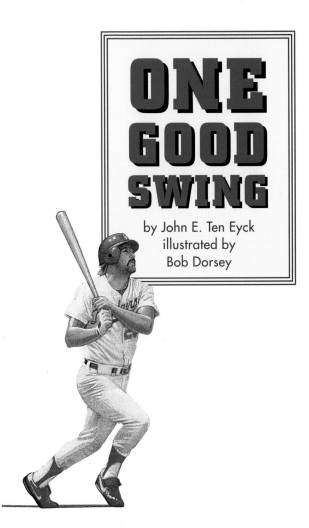

ONE GOOD SWING

by John E. Ten Eyck
illustrated by
Bob Dorsey

Scott Foresman

Editorial Offices: Glenview, Illinois • New York, New York
Sales Offices: Reading, Massachusetts • Duluth, Georgia
Glenview, Illinois • Carrollton, Texas • Menlo Park, California

The World Series has been the pride of major league baseball for almost a hundred years. The series is played each fall in front of millions of fans. The goal is for one team to win four out of seven games. When a team wins the World Series, the players become heroes for years to come.

Kirk Gibson sat inside the clubhouse. No one thought he would play in the game. But Kirk was convinced that he could help his team. In his heart, he knew he might have one good swing. Slowly, he rose to his feet.

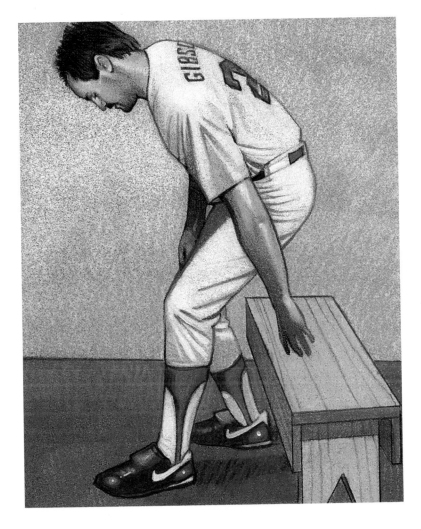

He picked up a bat and went to a room inside the stadium. There, he gradually began to swing the bat back and forth. Even though he was in pain, he told his coach that he could play.

But it seemed that Kirk would not get his chance. The Oakland pitcher, Dennis Eckersley, was on the mound. He was one of the best pitchers around.

The Dodgers had a man on first base. But they
had two outs. One more out and the Dodgers would
lose the game. Things were not looking good for
the Dodgers.

In a decision that surprised the fans, the Dodgers
sent Kirk out to bat. The crowd cheered as Kirk slowly
limped to home plate.

Kirk stood at home plate, in front of millions of fans. He was very courageous. He tried not to show he was in pain. As Kirk stared at Dennis Eckersley, the pitcher threw the ball. Kirk swung hard, but he hit a foul ball. Strike one!

Some fans began to wonder why he was even in the game. But Kirk didn't care. He just waited for the next pitch. When it came, Kirk swung his bat and hit another foul ball. Strike two!

Dennis Eckersley was now one pitch away from ending the game. However, Kirk was still convinced he had one good swing left. Now came the next pitch. Once again, Kirk hit a foul ball. But the fans began to think that Kirk might have a chance. The roar of the crowd gradually gave Kirk strength.

"One good swing," he repeated to himself. "One good swing."

Kirk stood in the batter's box. Eckersley's pitch missed the plate. Ball one! Kirk could hear his teammates shouting out to him, "You can do it, Kirk! Come on!"

Eckersley threw another pitch. Kirk swung and hit a foul ball. But with each swing, Kirk felt more and more ready to face the next pitch.

Eckersley threw another tough pitch. But it missed the plate. Ball two! The next pitch also missed the plate. Ball three!

Kirk waited for the next pitch. The Oakland pitcher threw his ball. Kirk knew he could hit it. He took a hard swing. Then, he felt the ball hit his bat.

Kirk looked up and saw the small white ball flying toward the fence in right field.

Kirk watched as the ball went over the fence. He had hit a home run! Gradually, he circled the bases. He was so excited he forgot about the pain in his leg.

The crowd jumped to its feet. The Dodgers had won the game by a score of 5–4! They were on their way to winning the World Series!

Kirk had helped his team win a big game with one good swing. And although Kirk didn't play in any of the remaining games of the World Series, he was able to celebrate when the Dodgers won the series that year.